Spotlight on™ Reading & Listening Comprehension
Fact & Opinion

by Paul F. Johnson & Carolyn LoGiudice

Skills	Ages
■ reading	■ 11 and up
■ listening	**Grades**
	■ 6 and up

Evidence-Based Practice

- Explicitly teaching and reinforcing inference-making leads to better outcomes in overall text comprehension, text engagement, and metacognitive thinking (Borné, Cox, Hartgering, & Pratt, 2005).

- Summarization is a skill that helps students identify main ideas, generalize what they've read, and recall information needed to answer comprehension questions (NRP, 2000).

- Instruction in comprehension can help students understand, remember, and communicate with others about what they read (NIFL, 2003).

- Teacher questioning improves students' learning from reading because it gives them a purpose for reading, focuses their attention on what they are to learn, helps them think actively as they read, encourages them to monitor their comprehension, and helps them review content and relate what they've learned to what they already know (NIFL, 2003).

- Effective listening strategies include (NCLRC, 2004):
  - Listening for details and main ideas
  - Predicting
  - Drawing inferences
  - Summarizing
  - Recognizing word-order patterns

Spotlight on Reading & Listening Comprehension Level 2 incorporates these principles and is also based on expert professional practice.

References
Borné, L., Cox, J., Hartgering, M., & Pratt, E. (2005). *Making inferences from text* [Overview]. Dorchester, MA: Project for School Innovation.

National Capital Language Resource Center (NCLRC). (2004). *Strategies for developing listening skills.* Retrieved June 15, 2009, from www.nclrc.org/essentials/listening/stratlisten.htm

National Institute for Literacy (NIFL). (2003). *Put reading first: The research building blocks for teaching children to read.* Retrieved June 15, 2009, from www.nifl.gov/nifl/publications.html

National Reading Panel (NRP). (2000). *Teaching children to read: An evidence-based assessment of the scientific research literature on reading and its implications for reading instruction–Reports of the subgroups.* Retrieved June 15, 2009, from http://www.nichd.nih.gov/publications/nrp/upload/smallbook_pdf.pdf

LinguiSystems

LinguiSystems, Inc.
3100 4th Avenue
East Moline, IL 61244
800-776-4332

FAX: 800-577-4555
Email: service@linguisystems.com
Web: linguisystems.com

Printed in the U.S.A.
ISBN 978-0-7606-0732-9

About the Authors

Paul F. Johnson, B.A., and **Carolyn LoGiudice**, M.S., CCC-SLP, are editors and writers for LinguiSystems. They have collaborated to develop several publications, including *Story Comprehension To Go*, *No-Glamour Sequencing Cards*, and *Spotlight on Reasoning & Problem Solving*. Paul and Carolyn share a special interest in boosting students' language, critical thinking, and academic skills.

In their spare time, Paul and Carolyn enjoy their families, music, gourmet cooking, and reading. Paul, a proud father of three children, also enjoys bicycling, playing music, and spending rare moments alone with his wife, Kenya. Carolyn is learning to craft greeting cards and spoil grandchildren.

Cover design by Jeff Taylor

Editing and page layout by Karen Stontz

Table of Contents

Introduction

Spotlight on Reading & Listening Comprehension was developed in 2005 to provide controlled reading materials for improving both overall and specific comprehension skills. Six separate booklets presented passages with readabilities that varied from grades 2.0 through 4.9 along with follow-up comprehension questions. Each booklet focused on one of these key reading comprehension skills:

- Characters & Actions
- Comparing & Contrasting
- Figurative Language & Exclusion

- Making Inferences & Drawing Conclusions
- Paraphrasing & Summarizing
- Sequencing & Problem Solving

Requests for a similar approach to reading comprehension skill-building that would be more appealing to older students has resulted in *Spotlight on Reading & Listening Comprehension, Level 2.* Not only are the readabilities of the passages increased in this series, but the content and visual elements are designed to appeal to older students reading below grade level.

Each booklet includes stories and comprehension questions for detecting the main idea, identifying details, and thinking about the vocabulary and semantics in the passage. In addition, each booklet includes comprehension questions for a specific skill area. This particular booklet features questions that require students to understand what is fact and what is opinion in what they have read. The other five booklets focus on these skill areas:

- Comparing & Contrasting
- Understanding Everyday Information
- Figurative Language

- Paraphrasing & Summarizing
- Making Inferences & Drawing Conclusions

The readability of the passages is controlled, based on the Flesch-Kincaid readability statistics. These statistics were revised in 2002; the new statistics yield a higher grade level in most cases than the previous ones. The range in readability is from grade levels 4.0 through 6.9. Each booklet includes eleven passages with the following readability ranges:

- Passages 1-3   Readability 4.0-4.9
- Passages 4-7   Readability 5.0-5.9
- Passages 8-11   Readability 6.0-6.9

The question pages for each passage also ask students to formulate questions about what they have read. The last task for each passage is a related writing prompt.

Use these passages for groups of students or individuals. Photocopy the material so each student has a copy. Encourage your students to highlight or underline key information as they read each passage and to jot down any questions they have.

Research proves that repeated readings improve reading comprehension and that three reads are usually sufficient repetition for a student to grasp the content, assuming a passage is at or below the student's reading competency level. We recommend training students to read a passage three times for adequate comprehension before trying to answer the comprehension questions.

The reading comprehension questions are similar to those found on classroom and national reading comprehension tests. Have your students read each possible answer for the multiple-choice questions before they select their answers.

As you present information to your students, model your own reading comprehension strategies. Talk about ways to rescan a passage to find key information and other tips that will help your students improve their reading competence and confidence.

We hope you will find *Spotlight on Reading & Listening Comprehension, Level 2* a welcome resource to help students understand and find satisfaction in what they read.

Paul and Carolyn

6

Story 1

Are kids too busy these days? They have a full plate with school, homework, and family events. Most adolescents also have church, club, or sports activities. Many also have part-time jobs. Some people think students don't have enough time to think, play, and hang with their friends. They don't get enough sleep. They don't have time to exercise. Between homework and scheduled activities, kids in middle school or high school have very little time for anything else.

Photo courtesy of istockphoto.com © Ana Abejon

"Sometimes it's hard to keep track of my schedule," notes Erin Lopez. "Besides being in the band, I'm a photographer for the yearbook. I also tutor kids in math and I babysit a lot. I have to check my calendar every day so I don't miss anything."

Dr. Martin, a child psychologist, says, "Being busy is just a fact of life. Kids should learn to deal with a full schedule. Kids who are used to being busy are better prepared to become busy adults." Dr. Martin has written a book to teach high school students to make the best use of their time. His book has sold over two million copies in just six months.

Some people want more time for themselves than others. Jamie Howe says, "I see plenty of kids in school. After school I like to make my own plans. I like to do things by myself, like read or play the piano. I like to be able to do what I want on my own time."

Some kids don't like to have to make their own schedules. "It's easier when I don't have to think about what to do," says Kip Lee. "I like being with my friends. If we are on the same sports team, we see each other every day. I don't have to plan anything."

Main Idea and Details

1. What is the main idea of this article?

    a. Kids don't have enough to do.

    b. Dr. Martin wrote a book for students.

    c. Students might be too busy.

2. What is Dr. Martin's profession?

    a. pediatrician

    b. child psychologist

    c. social worker

3. How do we know Dr. Martin's book is popular?

    a. He says so.

    b. It has sold many copies in a short time.

    c. both *a* and *b*

Vocabulary and Semantics

4. What does it mean that students **have a full plate**?

    a. They have a lot of food to eat.

    b. They eat a lot of meals at school.

    c. They have a lot to do.

5. What does it mean if something is a **fact of life**?

    a. It is something you can't change.

    b. It is something you can change easily.

    c. It is an unimportant detail.

Fact and Opinion

6. Which statement is a fact?

    a. Dr. Martin is out of touch with teens today.

    b. Dr. Martin's book is popular.

    c. High school students should read Dr. Martin's book.

7. Which statement is an opinion?

    a. Students should have time to exercise.

    b. Many kids have part-time jobs.

    c. Kids should be in charge of making their own schedules.

    d. both *a* and *c*

8. Do you agree or disagree with this opinion? Why?

    Students who aren't busy are lazy.

Asking Questions

Ask a question about remembering all the things you are scheduled to do.

Writing and Discussion Prompt ·······································

Do you have too much or too little on your plate? List the things you do often. Then explain why you are too busy, just busy enough, or not busy enough from your point of view.

Story 2

Photo courtesy of istockphoto.com © Alberto Pomares

Buying the right swimsuit can be a nightmare for girls! A good suit should fit well and be flattering. It should also let you move around comfortably without worrying about your suit or what part of your body shows. You want to have fun and look great at the beach or the pool, so pay attention when you shop for an awesome suit. The results will be worth the hassle!

Before you buy, it's important to try on lots of suits. Remember that suits look different on your body than they do on hangers or someone else. Narrow down your choices to the ones you like for color and style. Try each one on and move around in it. Bend over and jump up to see how the suit moves with your body. Then check out how you look in a three-way mirror.

A suit that ties will adjust to your body well. If the suit was tied before you tried it on, untie it to give yourself a custom fit. The same thing goes for suits with adjustable straps. You can readjust the straps to fit your body as well as possible. If the suit looks or feels small, try the next size larger. When you find the right fit and style, check out the brand. Most companies use the same fit year after year. If you find a brand of suit that flatters your body, is comfortable, and is priced within your budget, stick with that brand the next time.

Main Idea and Details

1. What is the main idea of this article?

   a. Boys don't have to worry about their swimsuits.

   b. There are tips to help you buy a good swimsuit.

   c. Don't buy a suit too big to fit well.

2. What kind of mirror is the most helpful when you buy a swimsuit?

   a. a three-way mirror

   b. one that magnifies

   c. a hand-held mirror

3. What style of suit is easy to adjust to your body?

   a. a one-piece suit

   b. a suit with thick fabric that stretches

   c. a suit that ties

Vocabulary and Semantics

4. What does **narrow down your choices** mean?

   a. Choose the slimmest suits.

   b. Choose just a few of all the suits you like.

   c. Lay out all your choices on the floor to help you decide.

   d. both *b* and *c*

5. True or false? A custom fit is one that seems as though someone made it just for your body.

Fact and Opinion

6. Which statement is an opinion?

   a. You can adjust straps to suit your body.

   b. Most swimsuit companies don't change the fit of their suits.

   c. Your swimsuit should flatter your body.

7. Which statement is a fact?

   a. You should try on lots of suits before you buy one.

   b. You can see yourself from different angles in a three-way mirror.

   c. Girls want to look good and have fun at the beach.

   d. both *a* and *b*

8. Do you agree or disagree with this opinion? Why?

   The way you look in a suit is more important than the price of the suit.

Asking Questions

Ask a question about making a wise choice when you buy a suit for the beach.

Writing and Discussion Prompt ·····································

Write a letter to a swimsuit manufacturer. Suggest ways the company could sell more of their suits to people like you.

Story 3

Photo courtesy of istockphoto.com © Emrah TURUDU

How does a soap or a lotion company know that its product is safe for your skin? How does a drug company know that its drugs are safe for you? They all need to test their products. Many times these tests are done on animals. U.S. firms test products on more than 20 million animals each year. They use rabbits, mice, monkeys, and other animals. The tests make sure products are safe for us.

Animal tests have saved many lives. They have helped scientists make vaccines and new drugs to keep us healthy. That was how we got rid of bad diseases like polio and smallpox. Many people think it's not fair to test animals. Many animals die or suffer because of these tests. PETA (People for the Ethical Treatment of Animals) is one group that wants to ban all animal testing.

Readability 4.7

Main Idea and Details

1. What is the main idea of this article?

   a. Animals are used to test drugs and products for humans.

   b. PETA is against animal testing.

   c. Polio is not a threat to health anymore.

2. What does PETA want to do?

   a. test more animals

   b. raise more animals for testing

   c. ban animal testing

3. True or false? Fewer than 20 million animals are tested every year in the U.S.

Vocabulary and Semantics

4. Which word is not a synonym for **ethical**?

   a. moral

   b. legal

   c. right

5. Which word is a synonym for **ban**?

   a. forbid

   b. expand

   c. support

   d. both *a* and *c*

Fact and Opinion

6. Which statement is a fact?

    a. All animals are hurt by animal testing.

    b. Some animals are hurt by animal testing.

    c. No animals are hurt by animal testing.

7. Which statement is an opinion?

    a. PETA is against animal testing.

    b. Rabbits and mice are often used for animal testing.

    c. Human life is more important than animal life.

    d. none of the above

8. Do you agree or disagree with this opinion? Why?

    We don't need animal testing to make sure new drugs or products are safe for humans.

Asking Questions

Ask a question about using animals to test new drugs or products.

Writing and Discussion Prompt ·······························

Is it important to test skin care products and medicines before they are available to the public? Explain your opinion in a letter to the editor of your local newspaper.

Story 4

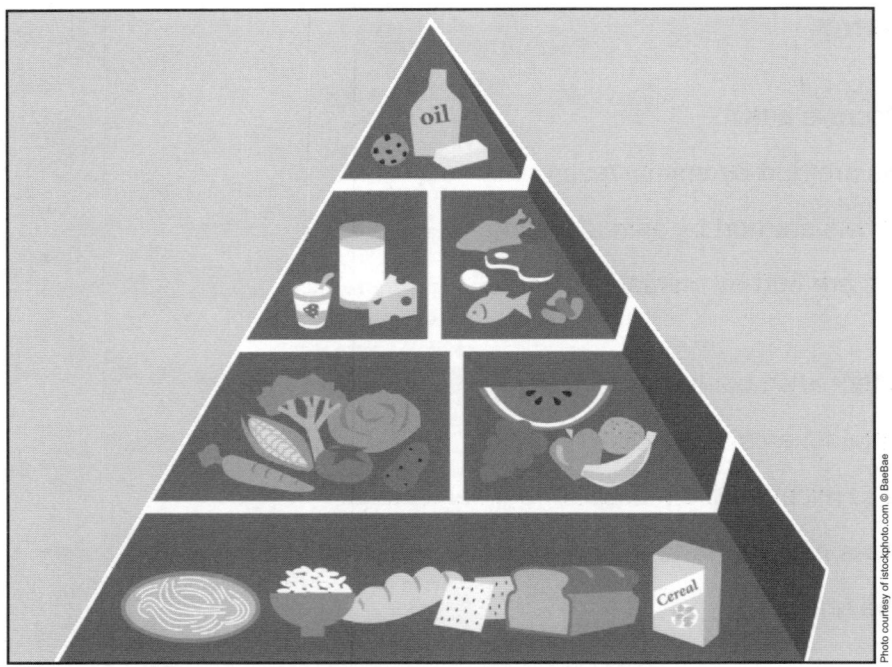

Ms. Kelsey is the new dietician for our school this year. She is in charge of preparing and cooking lunch for us.

The first thing Ms. Kelsey did was check out our menu. After her review, she made some changes. "There were too many starchy foods and not enough vegetables before," reported Ms. Kelsey. She replaced spaghetti and pizza with veggie burgers and raw carrots. Frozen yogurt replaced ice cream and pudding.

Obesity in children and adolescents is on the rise. It has more than doubled in the past 20 years. "Food isn't the only cause of this problem," says Ms. Kelsey, "but a healthy diet can help students avoid gaining too much weight."

Some students think the menu changes are fine. Other students wish we still had pizza and ice cream. Principal Rey noted, "It's almost impossible to make everyone happy about our lunch menu. I think we should just leave it up to Ms. Kelsey."

Good luck, Ms. Kelsey!

Main Idea and Details

1. Which is the best title for this article?

   a. Healthy Changes to School Lunch Menu

   b. Ms. Kelsey Carries Too Much Weight

   c. Where Is Our Pizza?

2. What is Ms. Kelsey's job?

   a. school nurse

   b. school principal

   c. school librarian

   d. none of the above

3. True or false? Ms. Kelsey changed the menu to add more foods with starch.

Vocabulary and Semantics

4. What does it mean if something is **on the rise**?

   a. It is going up a hill.

   b. It is happening more often.

   c. It is happening less often.

5. Which of these foods are **starchy** foods?

   a. potatoes

   b. bread

   c. spaghetti

   d. none of the above

   e. all of the above

Fact and Opinion

6. Which statement is a fact?

    a. Child obesity has more than doubled.

    b. Ms. Kelsey should be in charge of the school menu.

    c. Students should eat more raw vegetables.

7. Which statement is an opinion?

    a. It is impossible to make everyone happy with the school menu.

    b. Some students like the menu changes.

    c. Ms. Kelsey is the new school dietician.

8. Do you agree or disagree with this opinion? Why?

    Schools should only serve healthy foods with low sugar, low fat, and low salt.

Asking Questions

Ask a question about students deciding what should be on the school menu.

Writing and Discussion Prompt

Write a note to Ms. Kelsey. Tell her your favorite healthy foods and ask her to include them on the school menu. Explain why these foods are good for students.

Story 5

Photo courtesy of istockphoto.com © Paul Piebinga

In the past, adolescent girls looked at girls in their community to pick role models for how they wanted to look. There were few magazines for teens and there was no TV. Movie stars were mostly adults. Real girls were the best models around.

Now there are thin, beautiful teen models and stars everywhere. Teen magazines, TV shows, and movies feature trim teens with perfect skin and hair. That puts more pressure than ever on girls to look great.

Surveys show that looking "normal" is very important to girls, but there are many ideas about what's normal. The Girl Scout Research Institute learned that one-third of girls consider themselves too fat or too thin. In fact, only 16% of girls aged 6 to 19 are obese. That is a high number that causes concern for diabetes and other weight disorders, but many girls who think they are "fat" are just fine.

How do you know what's best for your body? Check with your doctor. Be active and eat healthy foods. Imitate active girls with good health habits. Most important, think about how you want to look for yourself, not for someone else's happiness.

Readability 5.5
Copyright © 2007 LinguiSystems, Inc.

Main Idea and Details

1. What is the main idea of this article?

   a. It is good to be thin.

   b. There is pressure for girls to look like stars.

   c. Most diets don't work well.

2. True or false? There are more adolescent stars today than there were years ago.

3. What percent of girls aged 6 to 19 are considered obese?

   a. 33%

   b. 25%

   c. 16%.

Vocabulary and Semantics

4. What is a **role model**?

   a. a part in a movie

   b. something with pieces that you put together

   c. someone you try to be like

5. Which of these words is not a synonym for **imitate**?

   a. mimic

   b. imagine

   c. copy

Fact and Opinion

6. Which statement is an opinion?

   a. Many teen models today are thin.

   b. Girls shouldn't worry about how they look.

   c. A doctor can tell you if your body weight is healthy.

7. Do you agree or disagree with this opinion? Why?

   If your parents are overweight, you will be overweight by the time you become an adult.

8. Do you agree or disagree with this opinion? Why?

   Movie stars make the best role models for how girls should look.

9. Do you agree or disagree with this opinion? Why?

   It is not important for students to be physically active.

Asking Questions

Ask a question about pressure on boys to look like male stars or athletes.

Writing and Discussion Prompt •••••••••••••••••••••••••••••••

Write your best tips for developing and keeping a good body image, even if your image is different from what your friends think it should be.

Story 6

Worried about acne on your face? Worry no more! ProClear is guaranteed to clear up acne or your money back.

ProClear fights the cause of acne, not just the surface problems. This revolutionary preparation was developed by a team of five dermatologists. Testing on 2,000 teens proved that ProClear does not irritate or dry the skin. Money can't buy a better acne treatment. You'll love the way your face looks in just two days!

We are positive you'll get great results with ProClear. If you don't, we'll refund your money. That's an incredible offer!

If you order ProClear now, you'll get a free facial cleanser that complements ProClear. Pay just $79.95 for a four-ounce bottle of ProClear repair lotion and a two-ounce jar of moisturizer and get ProClean FREE! You'll have beautiful skin in no time!

Main Idea and Details

1. What is the main idea of this article?

    a. Buy ProClear.

    b. Acne is not a problem.

    c. Everyone has acne.

2. Who developed ProClear?

    a. psychologists

    b. pharmacists

    c. dermatologists

3. How much does a bottle of ProClear lotion and a jar of moisturizer cost?

    a. under $50

    b. under $60

    c. under $70

    d. none of the above

Vocabulary and Semantics

4. What does this sentence mean? **Money can't buy a better acne treatment**.

    a. There is no better acne treatment, no matter what it costs.

    b. You don't have enough money to buy another acne treatment.

    c. both *a* and *b*

5. What is a **revolutionary product**?

    a. a product that was developed during the American Revolution

    b. a product that will bring about a major change

    c. a product that moves in a circular pattern

Fact and Opinion

6. Which statement is a fact?

    a. ProClear is revolutionary.

    b. ProClear does not dry the skin.

    c. ProClear will make your face beautiful.

7. Which statement is an opinion?

    a. You will get great results from using ProClear.

    b. ProClear has a money-back guarantee.

    c. ProClear was tested on 2,000 teens.

    d. none of the above

8. Do you agree or disagree with this opinion? Why?

    ProClear is a great acne product.

9. Do you agree or disagree with this opinion? Why?

    Any acne treatment developed by dermatologists must be good.

Asking Questions

Ask a question about acne problems or treating acne.

Writing and Discussion Prompt ·································

Imagine that you tried ProClear and it didn't work well for you. Write to ProClear to get your money back. Mention anything in the ad that wasn't true from your experience.

Story 7

How many times does the average adult in the United States expect to get married? Glynn Wolfe was listed in the Guinness Book of Records as the "Most Married Man in the World." He was married 29 times before he died at age 88. His longest marriage lasted for seven years; his shortest marriage lasted just 19 days.

Glynn's last wife, Linda Essex, probably married him as a publicity stunt. She had previously been married 23 times herself. A European news magazine helped to stage the event after the couple was together for one week.

It is not clear how many children Glynn had. The only known child was John Wolfe, from Glynn's 14th marriage. Others claim that Glynn had 19 children, 40 grandchildren, and 19 great-grandchildren. In any case, Glynn died alone. No one claimed his body or paid for his funeral. It's a pity Glynn was so alone.

Reporters asked John Wolfe why his dad had married and divorced so many women. John said his dad was "picky" and "stubborn." Glynn divorced one wife for eating sunflower seeds in bed!

Main Idea and Details

1. What is the main idea of this article?

   a. Glynn Wolfe was an unusual person.

   b. It is sad that Glynn Wolfe died alone.

   c. It's easy to get a divorce.

2. How many times was Glynn Wolfe married?

   a. 19

   b. 22

   c. 29

3. What official record did Glynn Wolfe hold?

   a. Most Charming Man

   b. Most Great-Grandchildren

   c. Pickiest Husband

   d. none of the above

Vocabulary and Semantics

4. What does it mean to do something as a **publicity stunt**?

   a. You do something you want everyone to know about.

   b. You do something so you can be in the news, not because you want to do it.

   c. both *a* and *b*

5. Which word is a synonym for **picky**?

   a. particular   c. fussy

   b. harsh   d. both *a* and *c*

Fact and Opinion

6. Which statement is a fact?

    a. A marriage that lasts only 19 days is too short.

    b. Glynn Wolfe had many children from different wives.

    c. No one claimed Glynn Wolfe's body when he died.

7. Which statement is an opinion?

    a. Glynn Wolfe's relatives should have claimed his body.

    b. Glynn Wolfe earned a record in the *Guinness Book of Records*.

    c. Glynn's last wife had also been married many times.

8. Do you agree or disagree with this opinion? Why?

    There should be a limit to the number of times a person can be divorced or married.

9. Do you agree or disagree with this opinion? Why?

    Stubborn people are hard to get along with.

Asking Questions

Ask a question you would like to have asked Glynn Wolfe before he died.

Writing and Discussion Prompt ·····································

What personal qualities or behaviors would help you to have a good relationship for a long time with someone you love?

Story 8

Do students cheat on tests? Seventy percent of high school students cheat, according to several studies over the past few years. Many students plagiarize, especially from the Internet. Some students copy from others during tests. Other students conceal notes to use during exams.

Cheating is not new. What's new is that more students consider cheating okay. Some blame the Internet and cell phones for making it easier to cheat. Others blame society for cheating in business, politics, sports, and other areas. In *The Cheating Culture*, author David Callahan wrote, "It's the normalization of cheating. Everybody's doing it. And if you don't, you feel like a chump."

There is more pressure than ever to get into good schools. That means getting good grades in high school is crucial. One principal said, "If I call parents about their child cheating, they are more upset about the kid's record than the cheating."

Some schools are trying to turn the tide. Through honor councils, classroom talks, news bulletins, and "no cheating" campaigns, schools are trying to honor honesty and discourage cheating.

Main Idea and Details

1. What is the main idea of this article?

   a. All students cheat today.

   b. Honest students don't cheat.

   c. Many students think it is okay to cheat.

2. What percent of high school students cheat?

   a. over 90%

   b. more than 50%

   c. less than 50%

   d. none of the above

3. True or false? Students didn't cheat in high school until ten years ago.

Vocabulary and Semantics

4. Which word is a synonym for **plagiarize**?

   a. copy

   b. punish

   c. publicize

5. What does it mean to **turn the tide**?

   a. to hold back the water when the ocean tide changes

   b. to make trouble for someone by getting them into hot water

   c. to reverse a trend or the way something is happening

Fact and Opinion

6. Is this a fact or an opinion?

   David Callahan wrote a book about cheating among high school students.

7. Is this a fact or an opinion?

   One way schools try to stop the cheating is to have students discuss cheating and honesty.

8. Do you agree or disagree with this opinion? Why?

   Students need to cheat to get good grades.

9. Do you agree or disagree with this opinion? Why?

   More students cheat today than they did years ago.

Asking Questions

Ask a question about punishing students who cheat.

> ### Writing and Discussion Prompt ································
>
> Imagine you wrote a book that has been published. You just learned that high
> school students are copying parts of your book for their reports in school. Most
> of these students don't cite you as the author of this material. Write a letter to
> these students to tell them your opinion about what they've done with your work.

Story 9

Photo courtesy of istockphoto.com © David Lewis

Pillow fights used to be something you did in pajamas with your good friends or your family. Recently a craze for public pillow fighting has swept the globe. It's considered a fun way to release tension and relieve stress through harmless physical activity. These fights can last just a few minutes or up to several hours.

In June 2006, hundreds of people participated in a mass pillow fight in Israel. There was just one simple rule: Keep your head low or be knocked down. The police were prepared to step in if necessary, but the event was peaceful and no one was hurt.

Word of large pillow fight events spreads quickly on the Web. This technique is called "smartmobbing." It's the best way to spread news about coming events anywhere in the world.

Flash mob pillow fights have increased lately. There have been mob pillow fights in France, Spain, Australia, Canada, Germany, the U.S., and other countries.

Readability 6.5
Copyright © 2007 LinguiSystems, Inc.

Main Idea and Details

1. What is the main idea of this article?

   a. Pillow fighting is not dangerous.

   b. Group pillow fighting has become popular.

   c. Pillow fights relieve stress.

2. How long are mob pillow fights?

   a. anywhere from a few minutes to several hours

   b. less than a minute

   c. more than ten hours

3. True or false? Pillow fighting is dangerous.

Vocabulary and Semantics

4. Which word is not a synonym for **craze**?

   a. fad

   b. trend

   c. craving

5. What does it mean if something **sweeps the globe**?

   a. It makes the world cleaner and less polluted.

   b. It is a contagious disease.

   c. People all over the world know about it quickly.

Fact and Opinion

6. Which statement is a fact?

   a. There are few rules for mob pillow fighting.

   b. People shouldn't hit each other, even with pillows.

   c. The best pillows are filled with goose feathers or down.

7. Which statement is an opinion?

   a. There are better ways to relieve stress than pillow fighting.

   b. Pillow fighting is fun.

   c. both *a* and *b*

   d. none of the above

8. Do you agree or disagree with this opinion? Why?

   Pillow fighting should be done indoors.

9. Do you agree or disagree with this opinion? Why?

   Only two people should pillow fight at a time.

Asking Questions

Ask a question about medical attention that should be available during a group pillow fight.

Writing and Discussion Prompt ·····························

List two things a group could do to relieve tension or stress. Then explain how each way is like or unlike group pillow fighting. Finally, state your opinion about the best way for a group to relieve tension and explain your reason or reasons.

Story 10

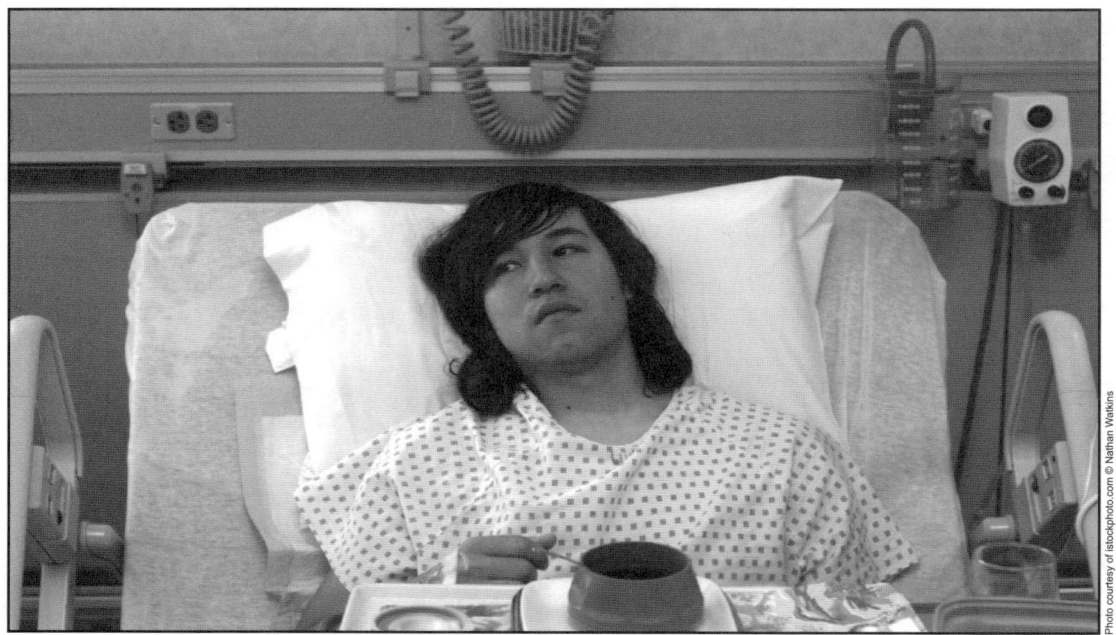

Who are smarter about their health, men or women? According to most women, men act like babies when they get sick. Lindsay Evergreen was a nurse in a hospital for 23 years. According to her, male hospital patients make almost twice as many requests of nurses as females with similar conditions. "When men are sick, they lie in bed and want to be waited on hand and foot," Evergreen said.

When it comes to heart health, maybe women should act more like men. A study by the University of Michigan found that women who have heart attacks are slower to get help than men. They are also less likely to improve their health.

Steven Erickson and others interviewed 348 men and 142 women who had suffered heart attacks. These patients were asked about their medication and their symptoms. The women were taking more medication and had more symptoms, yet they rated the seriousness of their disease the same as the men did. The women didn't consider their heart disease a big problem. Maybe their health would improve if they acted more like men!

Main Idea and Details

1. Which is the best title for this article?

   a. Sick Men Are Babies

   b. Who Act Smarter, Men or Women?

   c. Heart Disease Is Increasing

2. What was different about the men and women heart attack patients?

   a. The men stayed in the hospital less time than the women.

   b. The women worried more about their heart disease than the men.

   c. The women had more symptoms and took more medicine.

3. Which group studied men's and women's attitudes about having heart attacks?

   a. the University of Pennsylvania

   b. the University of Rochester

   c. the University of New York

   d. none of the above

Vocabulary and Semantics

4. What does it mean to be **waited on hand and foot**?

   a. You have to stand to eat or get help from a nurse.

   b. You don't need to do anything for yourself.

   c. You wait a long time for medical attention.

5. Which word is a synonym for **requests**?

   a. demands   c. hopes

   b. dreams   d. both *a* and *b*

Fact and Opinion

6. Which statement is a fact?

   a. The patients in the study were asked about their medication and their symptoms.

   b. Men act like babies when they get sick.

   c. Women consider heart disease a huge problem.

7. Which statement is an opinion?

   a. Researchers interviewed 348 men and 142 women.

   b. Sick men want to stay in bed and be waited on.

   c. Women with heart attacks take more medicine than men with heart attacks.

   d. none of the above

8. Do you agree or disagree with this opinion? Why?

   Women don't get as concerned about their health as men.

Asking Questions

Ask a question about recovering from a heart attack.

Writing and Discussion Prompt ·····························

Imagine you know you are going to be sick for a few days. Write instructions for how your family should act toward you while you are sick.

Story 11

Photo courtesy of istockphoto.com © Vidar Thorlaksson

On June 8, 793, a group of strange-looking ships approached a small island near England. Each ship carried 100 men. Rowers used long oars to move the boats. The other men were warriors wearing body armor and metal helmets. When the ships landed, the warriors streamed onto the island, carrying axes and swords. This unexpected attack was the first of many along the coastal areas of Europe. The inhabitants of small coastal villages most likely dreaded seeing Viking ships approach. The Vikings looted such villages and took their treasures home. These warriors had no fear. For 300 years, they raided wherever their ships could travel.

It was inevitable that Vikings would sail across the Atlantic Ocean. Their shipbuilders were the best in the world. Their speedy ships had special hulls that allowed them to ride over waves instead of plowing through them. They had huge sails and up to 50 long oars to keep them moving swiftly. Thanks to their excellent shipbuilders, Viking explorers were the first Europeans to reach North America.

Main Idea and Details

1. What is the main idea of this article?

    a. Viking warriors feared fighting on land.

    b. Viking shipbuilders were important for the success of Viking raids.

    c. Viking ships had many oars for rowing, so they could travel far away.

2. How long did Viking warriors raid the coastal areas of Europe?

    a. about 300 years

    b. about 400 years

    c. about 500 years

3. True or false? Viking warriors had no guns for weapons.

Vocabulary and Semantics

4. Which word is not a synonym for **looted**?

    a. discovered

    b. pillaged

    c. robbed

    d. both *b* and *c*

5. Which word is a synonym for **inevitable**?

    a. impossible

    b. unlikely

    c. certain

6. True or false? If you have no fear, then you are fearless.

Fact and Opinion

7. Which statement is a fact?

    a. Viking shipbuilders were the best in the world.

    b. Viking warriors were grateful to Viking shipbuilders.

    c. Viking warriors wore protective gear when they fought.

8. Which statement is an opinion?

    a. It was inevitable that Vikings would sail across the Atlantic Ocean.

    b. Vikings made unexpected attacks.

    c. Viking explorers were the first Europeans to reach North America.

9. Do you agree or disagree with this opinion? Why?

    Viking warriors were braver than the people the Vikings raided in small villages.

10. What opinion do you think the Vikings had about the villages they raided? Explain your reasons.

Asking Questions

Ask a question about becoming a Viking warrior.

Writing and Discussion Prompt ·······························

Imagine you live on a small island off the coast of England during the time of the Viking raids. Your island has not been raided yet. Write at least three things the people on your island could do to prepare for a Viking attack.

Readability 6.9

Answer Key

Story 1
1. c
2. b
3. b
4. c
5. a
6. b
7. d
8. Answers will vary.

Story 2
1. b
2. a
3. c
4. b
5. true
6. c
7. b
8. Answers will vary.

Story 3
1. a
2. c
3. false
4. b
5. a
6. b
7. c
8. Answers will vary.

Story 4
1. a
2. d
3. false
4. b
5. e
6. a
7. a
8. Answers will vary.

Story 5
1. b
2. true
3. c
4. c
5. b
6. b
7. Answers will vary.
8. Answers will vary.
9. Answers will vary.

Story 6
1. a
2. c
3. d
4. a
5. b
6. b
7. a
8. Answers will vary.
9. Answers will vary.

Story 7
1. a
2. c
3. d
4. c
5. d
6. c
7. a
8. Answers will vary.
9. Answers will vary.

Story 8
1. c
2. b
3. false
4. a
5. c
6. fact
7. fact
8. Answers will vary.
9. Answers will vary.

Story 9
1. b
2. a
3. false
4. c
5. c
6. a
7. c
8. Answers will vary.
9. Answers will vary.

Story 10
1. b
2. c
3. d
4. b
5. a
6. a
7. b
8. Answers will vary.

Story 11
1. b
2. a
3. true
4. a
5. c
6. true
7. c
8. a
9. Answers will vary.
10. Answers will vary.